# The Ro[...]
# in Yorks[...]

by

## Arthur Raistrick
Ph.D. M.Sc.

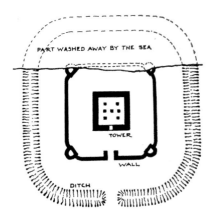

PART WASHED AWAY BY THE SEA

TOWER

WALL

DITCH

**DALESMAN BOOKS**
**1974**

**25p.**

## THE DALESMAN PUBLISHING COMPANY LTD., CLAPHAM, (via Lancaster), YORKSHIRE

**First Published 1960**
**Fourth Edition 1972**
**Reprinted 1974**

©     The Dalesman Publishing Company Ltd., 1960, 1974

ISBN : O 85206 140 4

Above : Labyrinth design of a tessellated pavement from the Roman villa of Harpham, East Yorkshire.

Title page : Plan of the Roman signal station at Scarborough Castle.

Printed in Great Britain by
GEO. TODD & SON,
Marlborough Street, Whitehaven.

# 1. The Brigantian Background of 74 A.D.

THE administrative area, Yorkshire, with its three Ridings, was an Anglo-Saxon creation and we can hardly speak of a "Yorkshireman" before about the seventh century A.D. if we are to observe a literal accuracy. None the less the country that is now Yorkshire was, for many centuries before being so named, occupied by people whose blood may in small part be mingled with that of some of the Anglian settlers and can have contributed its small share to the character of the dalesman.

Whether or not this is so, we can learn with interest of these peoples who lived here before the Romans, who joined with or defied the Romans, and who remained to occupy the country when the Romans left. A few names stand out to which we can give life and character and a study of remains, still to be seen on the hills and in our museums, can illuminate them with a little of the everyday life which they lived.

In this book it is proposed to sketch the story of the Brigantes and the Romans during those centuries of momentous events which stretch approximately between the first century B.C. and the fifth century A.D.

Although the story starts in what is correctly called the prehistoric period, it is only the later fringes that form a prelude to history, and there were many centuries, even millenia, of earlier pre-history which had passed before the Iron Age began. Many different groups of people had settled in the country, mingled their blood and cultures, passed through the ages of flint and stone and bronze before those arrived which formed the several tribes of the Iron Age peoples. East Yorkshire was occupied by the Parisii, and the Brigantes, a tribe of "Hillmen" claimed the mid and north Pennines as their territory and soon entered vividly into the story of the Roman settlement of the north.

Who were the Brigantes? is a question we can legitimately ask. We must turn back to about the fourth century B.C. when invaders from the Continent introduced new elements of culture into the south of England; the fusion of this, which we call the Hallstat culture, with that already local to the south, introduced the Iron Age "A" in which life was based upon arable farming and included a knowledge of pottery and textiles. There are three types of sites associated with these people, hill top forts, hut circles with small fields, and defended villages. Much of the Iron Age settlement of the Pennines seems to be of this Iron Age "A" type, though it is later in actual date.

In the third century B.C. there was a further invasion of people from the Continent, the La Tene folk, who brought with them from the homelands around Lake Constance a considerable artistic skill, particularly in metal working.

3

One group of these La Tene settlers reached into Craven, and some of the objects associated with them are the fine bronze torc or necklet found nearly a century ago at Embsay, the decorated sword and scabbards at Flasby and near Ripon, and probably the famous Swastika rock carving at Ilkley.

The La Tene people were largely absorbed into the Iron Age "A" population and from this mingling emerged the northern folk whom we know as Brigantes. The name probably originates from the place from which they came on the Continent, around the town still called Brigenz, and it was the name by which they were known to the Romans.

We can say little of the Brigantes before the first century A.D., but early in that century they had developed a confederation of groups stretching over the Pennines from the Calder valley to the Tyne, and they had achieved a considerable degree of civilisation. Ptolemy, writing of Britain, gives a list of nine Brigantian towns, most of which have been identified. The Brigantes were ruled by a king or queen and had a gold coinage of their own, which they used in their trading along with a large number of the earlier Roman silver coins. Outside the towns the people lived either in small villages, farmsteads, or even in single huts with one or two fields and small enclosures and shelters for sheep and cattle.

The main part of the population was made up of small farmers living in hard conditions, and experiencing considerable poverty. The climate during the Iron Age was colder and wetter than at present. The valleys were largely filled with swamp and thickets and the only dry ground on which living was tolerable was provided by the principal outcrops of limestone or grit on the hillsides, and a few of the larger gravel mounds and ridges, most of which are moraines left from the Ice Age.

We have to look for the Iron Age remains on the plateau around Ingleborough, the Malham Moors, or the terraces of Wharfedale and the other dales where the Main or other limestones make a prominent feature. In East Yorkshire the chalk Wolds and some of the Jurassic hills of Cleveland provide equally good sites. Only a very few of the outstanding summits were used, such as Ingleborough, Castle Hill at Almondbury, and possibly Addlebrough, in Wensleydale, Eston Nab, and a few others, but many smaller prominences, particularly those in the junction of two streams, were favoured.

Let us look at one or two of the Iron Age sites and so get some idea of life and conditions at the beginning of the Roman period. We can take first a moderate sized family farm of an early type. The footpath from Arncliffe to Malham Moor, which goes up the east side of Cowside Beck and by Middle House, passes Dewbottoms at two miles from

Arncliffe. This is a small promontory between two grassy hollows, the path crossing the neck of it alongside a fairly large spring. The level summit of the promontory is about two acres in extent and is now partly covered by bare limestone, the soil having been eroded away. It is occupied by several fields the boundaries of which are now only low gravel banks with lots of limestone boulders in them, some of them fairly big. These banks are the collapsed footwalls of a stockaded fence.

Near the middle of the area and on a place where several enclosures meet, there is a large round hut. This is now a circular mound of large stones, hollow at the centre, but formerly it would be a massive stone wall two or three feet high, with posts set in it on which a thatched roof was carried. An exactly similar hut has been excavated near Middle House and that gives us an idea of what they were like. This hut would house the head of the family, and sons and others were probably housed in two or three similar but smaller huts seen along the field walls and on the next little promontory. There are a few still cruder shelters against another of the field walls, and some rather larger foundations, probably those of cattle sheds.

We can picture a family group with a few servants, about twenty people in all, living here raising a little oats on these and other small fields near at hand, breeding sheep and perhaps a few cattle, and doing a fair amount of hunting. It was a hard life on a very marginal subsistence level. This farm has many of the features of the Bronze Age farms of Wales which, like this one, remained in occupation with little change through the Iron Age. Larger settlements are common on the limestone area of Craven, and on many of the terraces of the Dales, such as those around Addlebrough in Wensleydale, and there are many sites on the limestones near Ravenstonedale in Westmorland.

A larger settlement can be seen not far from Dewbottoms on the Middle House Back Pasture, alongside the footpath from Middle House to Darnbrook. This is a collection of nearly twenty circular foundations of huts, protected by a stone bank and wall on one side and high limestone scarps on the other. It is a typical defended village site.

The population, though so scattered, was linked with that of the towns in the first century A.D., though we should fail to recognise any of the sites as towns in our present sense of the word. They were only larger villages in which there was a little less poverty and in which some degree of trading was carried on. Some of these town sites were chosen by the Romans for their forts, so that we know them now mainly through the numerous articles brought to light during the excavations around the Roman fort.

The names of Brigantian towns were Vinnovium (Binchester near Bishop Auckland), Caturactonium (Catterick), Isurium (Aldborough), Olicana (Ilkley), Eboracum (York). Camoludunum (Almondbury near Huddersfield) was not made into a Roman fort but may have been a capital of Brigantia during the Roman Conquest. Rigodunum was almost certainly the walled village which covers the summit of Ingleborough; Epiacum was probably the hill settlement of Black Rod, near Wigan, and the last of them, Calatum, is still unidentified. Aldborough was called by the Romans Isubrigantium, an indication that it was the capital town of the Brigantes during part of their period.

East of the Vale of York the contemporaries of the Brigantes were the tribe of Parisii, connected not with Central Europe but the Seine valley, where they gave their name to the city of Paris. Their culture included some customs different from those of the Brigantes, one of which was that of chariot burial. In these burials the body was accompanied by a chariot, horse harness, and weapons or ornaments. In one chariot burial on the Wolds, between Market Weighton and Beverley, the skeleton was that of a woman with the remains of the chariot (iron tyres, wheel hubs, lynch pins, harness rings, bits, etc.), an iron mirror and the bones of two pigs; other chariot burials frequently contain pig bones which seem to have had some special significance. This burial may have been that of a British queen like Boudicca of the Iceni or Cartimandua of the Brigantes. The only chariot burial on the Yorkshire Pennines is represented by a group of objects excavated at Stanwick in 1844. These included the harness of several horses, iron hoops from chariot wheels and many decorative articles of bronze. They were in a pit about 5ft. deep.

In 1829 a hoard of coins was found at Almondbury in which were eighteen British gold coins, of which five can still be seen in the York Museum. In 1893 another hoard was found at Honley which included five British silver coins, and others have been found at Lightcliffe and Keighley. The native coins have on them the following names of rulers — VOLISIOS, DUMNOVEROS (sometimes written DUMNOCOVEROS) and CARTIMANDUA, and it is now thought that Volisios was a king of Brigantia, Dumnocoveros his son and Cartimandua his daughter and heiress, who was queen of Brigantia at the time of the Roman Conquest.

Along with these British coins there were large numbers of Roman silver coins of various dates between 209 and 41 B.C., such as were in common use among Roman and native traders before the conquest. We must therefore think of the Iron Age Brigantes as having some contact with Roman traders in the towns to the south and east of their territory, and of being ruled by kings and queens, even though most of their population in the hills was scattered on small farms, living a life not far removed from acute poverty. The first invasion of Britain by Romans was that led by Julius Caesar in 55 B.C., but the Romans only just crossed the Thames and secured no footing further north. For nearly a century no further attempt was made towards a military conquest, and it is during this century that the Roman traders made their contacts with Brigantia and the North.

In 43 A.D. the Romans began their second conquest and subdued the south and south east, coming as far north as Colchester and making friendly relations with the British of the south Midlands. In A.D. 47-48 Ostorius Scapula, then the Governor of Britain, advanced his troops north westwards towards Chester to separate the Pennines from Wales and the Brigantes from the Silures, the natives of the Welsh borders. He had made some sort of approach or pact with the Brigantes but this was resented by many of them so that there were already two strong parties in Brigantia, pro-Roman and anti-Roman. In A.D. 51, according to Tacitus "Caratacus (leader of the Silures) seeking the protection of Cartimandua, Queen of the Brigantes, was put in chains and delivered to the conquerors, nine years after the beginning of the war in Britain."

Cartimandua had married a native Brigantian, Venutius, whom Tacitus described as pre-eminent in military skill. His hatred of the Romans led to many quarrels with Cartimandua and he became the leader of a resistance movement against the Romans. In reprisal Cartimandua captured his brothers and kinsfolk and in 51 A.D., when Cartimandua added to all this provocation by the betrayal of Caratacus, Venutius left her and was divorced.

The Roman soldiers were again called to her aid and for ten or twelve years there was unrest and guerilla fighting in Brigantia, in attempts to defeat and eliminate the anti-Roman party now led by Venutius and steadily increasing in numbers and power. Cartimandua sought refuge with the Romans and Venutius gathered the Brigantes in the western parts of Yorkshire and established his headquarters in the walled "town" on Ingleborough summit.

This "town" is an area of about 450 feet by 490 feet, a four sided figure with the shape of the hill summit. Within the wall there is a large number of hut circle foundations of stone, still to be seen under the thinner turf, and over 20 of them clearly seen in a good air photograph. From this stronghold he consolidated the Brigantian rebels into a major force capable of building the Stanwick Park defences and of meeting the Roman attack in 74 A.D.

It was obvious to Venutius that the Romans would sooner or later make a large scale attack upon him and his followers, so he planned to be in a position to meet them on ground chosen by himself and prepared for the encounter.

7

In 69 A.D. he called in the help of other tribesmen, even some from Scotland, and at Stanwick in the North Riding constructed his great defences against a Roman attack.

Stanwick Park, five miles north of Richmond, is the most imposing of all the Brigantian sites, with its 850 acres surrounded by and divided by six miles of ditches and ramparts which in places are more than twenty feet high. The defences centre round Tofts Hill, a seventeen acres site enclosed by a bank and ditch, the bank being twenty-four feet high on the west side. This enclosure takes full advantage of a small but well defined hill on which excavation has uncovered the foundations of a circular hut and other evidence of an occupation in the middle years of the first century. The site has many of the features that might be described as those of a Brigantian hill fort. Soon after 55 A.D. extensive plans were started to increase the defended area by bringing within the circuit of new banks and ditches, a second and much larger area. A few years later this was again extended by a third area; in fact the work may have been almost continuous on the site.

The work is so vast that an army of all available men from the Brigantian area must have been almost continuously employed either in actual construction or in securing the large food supplies that were needed. It may be that much of the Brigantian population was moved into temporary camps in the Dales behind Stanwick, an area where small promontory earth-works are fairly common, and where many smaller natural sites are marked off by a ditch and bank.

Along with Stanwick there may have been some provision to hamper an attack from the south, and it seems likely that the great work of the Ta Dyke at the head of Scale Park above Kettlewell belongs to this work. It is a great ditch, a large part of it rock cut like the ditches at Stanwick, with a bank and enclosures on the north side of it. It has long been a puzzle why this earthwork should appear to defend the wild moorlands from attack coming up the valley, but an outpost from the concentrations towards Stanwick would meet the case and solve the problem. Outlying works like the stone fort on Gregory near Grassington, and Addlebrough near Bainbridge, might well belong to this same plan and period.

The Roman legions under Petillius Cerialis were advanced against Stanwick before all the defences were completed, and in the great battle that took place, Venutius was defeated and many of his people were forced to retreat into the Dales. Following this defeat of 74 A.D. the great concentrations of Iron Age hutments, fields and "camps" around Ingleborough, Grassington and Settle, and in the western parts of the Dales, probably had their greatest expansion.

It was a custom of the Roman Empire to use prisoners of war and criminals as slave labour in the Imperial mines. Very soon after the arrival of the Romans in Britain, the mines of Charterhouse in Mendip, were producing lead with conscript slave labour. Pigs of smelted lead were exported to other parts of the Roman Empire but some were lost or stolen, and one of these which has been found on or near the mines bears the inscription : IMP. VESPASIAN. AVG. on the base and, on the side, BRIT. EX. ARG. VEB., and comes from the period 69-79 A.D. Another with the name and titles of the Emperor Claudius is dated to 49 A.D.

In Yorkshire many pigs of lead have been found, four of them within the Dales area and the others near Brough on Humber. In 1735 two pigs of lead were found on the side of an ancient trackway down Hayshaw Bank in the parish of Dacre. This track could be leading from Greenhow Hill to the Roman road to Boroughbridge. A countryman riding this way found the lead when his horse stumbled with its foot in the hole in which the lead was hidden. The pigs of lead had the inscription : IMP: CAES: DOMITIANO: AVG. COS: VII, and on one side BRIG. The seventh year of the consulship of Domitian is the year 81 A.D. and the word BRIG probably means "from the area of the Brigantes." Another pig of lead of TRAJAN date (A.D. 98-117) was found near Nussey Knott, four miles west of Hayshaw Bank, "hidden among the stones of the moor." The fourth was found at the Hurst Mines in Swaledale, and had an inscription of HADRIAN (A.D. 117-138).

It is not too much to assume that the mines at Greenhow Hill and at Hurst were well known to the Brigantes, as many fragments of lead and articles of lead have been found in their camps, and that the Romans soon developed these mines, using them as slave camps for the prisoners taken at Stanwick. The Brigantes must have fostered a hatred of these ruthless conquerors and taken every means of robbing and annoying them. We know that time after time they attacked the Roman forts, as we shall see later, and it is certain that these pigs of lead were hidden by native carriers, slaves, or by someone who had managed to steal them, and hidden them.

The Nussey Knott pig, well to the west of the mines and away from a Roman track, suggests theft more than an accidental loss. What happened to the man who hid the Hayshaw Bank pigs we shall never know. These may not have been the first or only pigs hidden, and it may have been his native friends and accomplices who should have removed them. Here are the materials for an imaginative reconstruction of a vivid story. The mines were worked by the Romans for two or three generations, but later were leased to natives and to freed slaves, who continued them.

There was a considerable trade in lead as the five pigs found at Brough on Humber, and the total of seventy pigs found at various parts of England indicate. Those found at Brough were from Derbyshire, all carrying the names of Roman citizens and the further distinguishing word LVT or LVTVD, meaning from the Lutudares, the tribe occupying Derbyshire.

Following the defeat of the Brigantes, Petillius established a centre of civilian government from which they could be kept in order and supervised. He created the town of Isurium at Aldborough near Boroughbridge. This was the most important civilian site in Yorkshire, and was the cantonal headquarters of the Brigantes. The town covered an area of fifty-five acres and, being only sixteen miles from York, could rest under the close supervision of the legionary commander there. In the middle of the second century the massive stone wall defences, one and a quarter miles in length, and with a wall eight to nine feet in thickness, were added, then again about 350 A.D. corner bastions were built to give additional strength.

# 2. The Roman Conquest
## (74 A.D. to Mid-Second Century)

IN 74 A.D. Petillius Cerialis was succeeded as governor of Britain by Sextus Julius Frontinus who, with the Brigantes more or less quiet in the North, could turn his force to the conquest of Wales, and thus establish a relatively peaceful frontier across the country between the two legionary fortresses of Chester and York. When Agricola became governor four years later, the Brigantes north of this line were a potential threat to his plans for the conquest of the north, so he started to build a series of roads and forts which would enclose them and keep them under constant supervision.

He began by building roads north from both York and Chester to the Tyne and Solway, probably employing a good deal of slave or conscripted native labour, as well as prisoners. The eastern road is partly obscured by later road work, as much of its line is used by the modern road. In a southern section from Doncaster to Castleford this is also the case, but north of Castleford the road is more recognisable as a prominent ridge, about twenty-four feet wide and in some places five feet high above the surrounding country.

This road passes through Aberford to Newton Kyme, to a fort at Long Brough on the south bank of the Wharfe. Parts of the wall of this fort can still be seen. From St. Helen's ford the road goes to Aldborough and in that part is called the Rudgate, but it is covered by the modern road.

The Rudgate follows a pre-Roman track and another native track was also used as the foundation for the Roman road which made the connection from York to a point south of Aldborough.

From Aldborough the road is continued northward as Leeming Lane to the fort at Catterick which is now covered by part of the race-course. From Catterick the road is called Watling Street, and it is now the main road to Scotch Corner. It continues to Piercebridge on the Tees, then by Lanchester to Corbridge on the Tyne. A branch road at Scotch Corner leads off to the west to cross Stainmore, where much of it is visible, and its line can then be traced to Carlisle. There were forts at Greta Bridge and Bowes, and the ramparts of another are still to be seen on the south side of the Stainmore road at Rey Cross.

A southern boundary road was made across the Pennines through Manchester, Castleshaw and Slack, with forts at all these places. Castleshaw was excavated in 1912 when an early fort, 360 feet by 300 feet, was found, which had earth ramparts and timber gateways and buildings. It dates from 79-80 A.D., and was in use for about ten years. Early in the second century it was replaced by a much smaller fort, 160 feet by 190 feet, with turf ramparts and timber gateways, but with a few stone buildings. The fort at Slack was similarly reduced in size when rebuilt later.

A second cross-Pennine road was built from York to Ribchester, through Skipton and Elslack, with a cross road from Aldborough through Ilkley to Manchester. It is on these cross roads that some of the best preserved portions are still to be seen. Where the Aldborough to Manchester road crosses Blackstone Edge, there is a fine piece of road sixteen feet wide, with its paving or large sandstone blocks held in position by a heavy kerb. The centre of the road has a continuous line of very large stones hollowed into a gutter, but it is suggested that the hollow was made by the wear and tear of a drag or skid, used as a brake on the chariots.

Where this road approaches the modern Halifax to Rochdale road and crosses Black Castle Clough, it is carried over the small stream by a bridge with two culverts of Roman date, but these have been rebuilt. A long stretch of this road can be seen on Blubberhouse Moor as a causeway still called "Watling Street." This clear section starts just below Round Hill and runs in a straight line for over five miles, being interrupted for about one mile, in crossing the valley just below Blubberhouses. The modern road to Harrogate is built on it from one mile east of Blubberhouses to the bend just before Kettlesing Head. This road bends near Round Hill and runs through Middleton Moor near March Ghyll Reservoir then as Parks Lane and Hardings Lane to the fort at Ilkley.

From Ilkley it goes over Rombalds Moor and crosses Airedale by Morton, south to the Calder, which it crossed at Sowerby and then south west to Blackstone Edge. In 1775 a large hoard of silver coins of all the emperors from Nero to Pupienus (54 A.D. to about 238 A.D.) was found near the road on Morton Bank. The coins had been buried in a metal chest, probably for safety during the troubles of the later third century, and never recovered by their owner.

The York to Ribchester road through Adel and over Otley Chevin passes through Ilkley, and along Draughton Moor side it is a very clearly marked way. It is joined by the Blubberhouse Moor road, probably in the neighbourhood of Addingham.

There was an important road on the west of the Pennines, going north from Ribchester to Bowland and eventually to Carlisle. From Ribchester it crosses the west end of Longridge Fell, goes through the Hodder valley and to the west of Slaidburn into Croasdale. Over the fells it keeps nearly north to cross the Wenning valley and then makes directly for Casterton, leaving the fort of Over Burrow some distance on the west of its line. The road keeps up the east side of the Lune and the Rawthey to near Brigflatts, then crosses back on to the east bank of the Lune around the foot of the Howgill Fells, to the fort of Low Barrow. From there it goes north to Old Penrith.

It is to the Agricolan plan of roads and forts that we owe most of the forts in Yorkshire except York and Malton, though all were rebuilt and modified in later periods. The general Roman plan was to surround the Brigantes by a framework of roads and forts and to man them with auxiliary forces conscripted from recently conquered people, keeping the Legions, which were made up of Roman citizens, in a few legionary fortresses in the rear. York was the headquarters of the IXth Legion, with about 6,000 men, and this was used as the base from which the auxiliaries, in companies of from 500 to 1,000 men, established the defensive and police forts associated with the road network.

Malton, like York, was founded by Petillius Cerialis but was used by Agricola to control East Yorkshire. The rectangular platform of the fort can be seen in the angle between the Derwent, the railway line, and the Pickering road. Like all the other sites, Malton was frequently rebuilt, but recent excavation has unravelled most of the story. The first fort with earthen ramparts and wood buildings was of large extent, about 22 acres, enough for a whole legion. Agricola replaced this by a much smaller fort, partly built of stone, and intended to protect York from the east. Early in the second century it was rebuilt, all in stone, but was reduced in importance and about 280 A.D. it was abandoned for a time. In the later period of the Roman occupation Malton became the centre of a large and peaceful civilian population, about which more will be said later.

The Romans were a very systematic people and worked to strict rules in nearly all matters, so that the forts, throughout the country follow a single plan with only minor local variations from it. For this reason all the Roman forts appear much alike at first sight and only careful study and excavation will reveal differences.

A person wishing to understand the general plan could not do better than to take a holiday along the Roman Wall and see there some of the larger forts like Housteads or Chesters, which are almost completely excavated, or the ones south of the Wall at Corbridge or South Shields. These remains, with the contents of the excellent museums on the site, will tell more of the life and conditions of the Roman forces in this country than a large amount of reading could do.

In general plan a fort was rectangular with a rampart and one or more ditches outside it. There were four gates, one in each wall, those in the shorter walls generally being central. The central feature of the fort was the Headquarters Building, fronting and connected to the main gate by a road, with a second road joining the two sidegates and crossing the fort in front of it.

Other official buildings, the Commandant's house, workshops, stores, etc., were right and left of the Headquarters Building and facing on the cross road. Much of the space behind these buildings in the two quarters between the roads was taken up by granaries, stables or barracks, and barracks often filled the other two quarters of the fort in the earlier examples. Many forts had a bath house just outside the ramparts and some had a civilian settlement where soldiers' families and others would live.

There are very few of the seventy forts of the Pennines and Wales where there now remains much to be seen beyond the line of the ramparts and ditches. Bainbridge is one of the best to visit. Situated on the summit of the small hill just outside the village, it has remained free from any subsequent building or damage, and its ramparts can be seen completely. Excavations are being carried out in the summer season by the archaeology department of Leeds University. The recently uncovered buildings can be seen along with the various finds which are housed in a museum on the site.

Elslack fort, though complete, is divided by a railway line at Elslack station, and nothing is to be seen but the nearly filled in ditch and the line of the ramparts. As in nearly all cases, the excavations made here had to be filled in and the ground restored to a usable pasture. A very well illustrated account of the excavations, both here and at Ilkley, is published in the **Yorkshire Archaelogical Journal.**

# Roman York

One of the principal cities of
the Roman province of
Britain

Above, left : Part of the 4th century fortress wall still standing in St. Leonard's. Above, right : Part of a skeleton found in Mount Vale in 1952; there is a coin in the mouth and a flagon at the shoulder. (Photos : Robin Hill). Opposite : York from the Walls. (Photo : John Edenbrow). Below : Dedication stone of a Temple of Serapis at York.

DEO · SANCTO
SERAPI
TEMPLVM · ASO
LO · FECIT
CL · HIERONY
MIANVS · LEG
LEG · VI · VIC

Ilkley fort is more than half covered by the church and many other buildings, and little can be seen there beyond the collection of remains in the Ilkley Museum.

At Aldborough there is more to see, though the remains are those of a Romano-British town and not of a fort. There are many tessellated pavements, remains of the city walls, the foundations and pavement of a basilica, and a wealth of objects. The town flourished in the third and fourth centuries, and was then probably the second largest Romano-British town in England. It was a centre of civil life and administration and represented a standard of life and comfort not to be found in any of the forts, but only in the larger fortresses like York and Malton.

Under the strict rules of the Roman Army, life in all the forts must have followed very much the same pattern and routine. The duties consisted mainly of patrolling the area and lengths of road consigned to its care, keeping the road safe, and giving shelter and convoy to the numerous travelling officials. Stores had to be brought into the fort, exercises held, and regular training continued.

The soldiers were mainly vegetarian, the basis of their diet being wheat, which was issued to them in the grain and ground by them as required, in stone querns. Wine and oil was used in fair quantity and must have been one of the larger imports. There seemed to be no shortage of pottery in any of the camps, some was made locally, as at Crambeck near Malton, and Holme-on-Spalding Moor, and finer tableware and glassware was imported from the Continent.

There was a small amount of trade with the quieter groups of natives, by which Roman objects found their way into native settlements, and no doubt from time to time there were hunting expeditions from the forts, after wild boar, and possibly wolves. The garrisons had some leisure time, and games of chance using dice and other articles were common. The religion was satisfied by regular observance and by numerous altars dedicated to emperors and gods.

The systematic occupation of the forts and roads did not last long. Excavation shows that many of the sites were soon neglected and abandoned following changes of plan in the northern campaign. In 115 A.D. there was a widespread and very serious revolt of the northern tribes and many of the forts were destroyed, some like Ilkley being burned down and many others having buildings torn down and destroyed. The revolt was serious enough for punitive expeditions to be sent from the Continent, and during these troubles the IXth Legion was either disgraced or almost eliminated, as it was replaced at York with the VIth.

Hadrian came to Britain in 122 A.D. and adopted a new plan which included the building of the Wall from the Solway to the Tyne, and a partial withdrawal from the south of

Scotland. It is probably to this period of revolt and resettlement that we must refer the earlier groups of Romano-British cave remains in Craven.

In the limestone area stretching from Ingleborough across to Wharfedale, there are many caves which on excavation have provided a large number of Romano-British objects. Most of these articles can be seen well displayed in the Pig Yard Museum, Town Head, Settle, in the care of Mr. T. Lord, jnr., who has done much to secure and preserve them. This collection is unique in the North of England and no account of Brigantian life can afford to neglect it.

The remains are of various dates but the largest and most important group belongs to about the first quarter of the second century. The caves appear to have been places of shelter and retreat with habitation sites and small fields close to them, where a similar suite of objects has been found.

The most interesting of the articles are the numerous bronze brooches of several types, many of them still bearing traces of coloured enamel decoration. There are "trumpet" brooches belonging to the period about 100 to 150 A.D., smaller penannular brooches, disc brooches, and, the most interesting and elaborate group of all of them, the dragon-esque brooches. All these are of comparable date and are regarded as of fairly local Brigantian origin and workmanship, probably being made near Brough under Stainmore. Bone was used for a large variety of things, needles, chisels, hooks, weavers' combs, dress fastenings, and even dice, and among the dress fastenings we must probably include the 'perforated bone spoons' which have given rise to so much speculation.

There are a number of well-carved bone spoons, the distinctive features of which are that the handle often has a carved head somewhat in the fashion of an apostle spoon, and that the bowl is perforated. The head may be a simple square with a pattern carved on it, or something more elaborate, even in one case a well carved bird; the bowl always has a hole in the middle.

Pottery was present in quantity, much of it of course native ware, but fragments of Samian were occasionally found, and at Dowkerbottom, a complete bowl. The iron objects include spear heads, knives, and many other tools and articles whose use is not now recognised. The whole picture which these remains present is one of unrest and of unusual conditions. It may be that the cave remains include plunder from some of the Roman forts which were attacked, particularly the ironwork and pottery, though the bronzes are a native product and they suggest a concentration in Craven of the craftsmen who kept alive the art traditions and skills through this troubled time.

**17**

The revolt seems to have quietened down, as Ilkley fort was rebuilt in 125 A.D., this time with a stone rampart. The defence of the Hadrianic wall from Tyne to Solway drew some of the troops from the Pennines, but the Sixth Legion at York and the Twentieth at Chester were sufficient for the policing of Brigantia.

Between 140 and 145 A.D. another wall from the Firth of Forth to the Clyde was built by Antoninus and more troops were drawn from the South Pennines and Wales to help out the Antonine garrisons. The protection afforded by the new frontier against the invasion of Brigantia from the north led to a short period of comparative prosperity among the Brigantes. By 154 A.D. however, the Brigantes broke out again in revolt against the weakened Roman overlordship, and were assisted by a simultaneous outbreak in Scotland and in the country between the two walls. Coins of Pius were issued in 155 A.D. to celebrate a victory in Britain which could only be the suppression of this revolt.

One important event which seems to belong to this period was the end of the Roman lead mining in the North. It is not too much to guess that the revolt was probably responsible for ending the slave and convict camps at the lead mines in Swaledale and at Greenhow, and whatever methods of punishment the Romans may have adopted, forced labour in those penal settlements was never resumed.

According to Pausanius this revolt was followed by the annexation of part of Brigantia by the Romans, probably the Vale of York between and around York and Boroughbridge. Sometimes during the second century this part was established as a "Colonia", an area of farms and estates on which the Romans and Romanised Brigantes were settled as farming colonists. The Roman buildings on Castle Hills, Northallerton, were occupied after 150 A.D. and the signs of civilian life, along with a dedicatory inscription, "Erected under the supervision of Flavius Hyginius, Centurion of the 6th Legion, the Victorious," shows that most of the Vale of York was now occupied by a Romano-British population under the supervision of the 6th Legion from York. There is evidence of Roman or Romanised populations during the second century at Whorlton, Guisborough and Whitby, but in general Cleveland was only thinly populated.

# 3.  A Time of Prosperity

## 150 A.D. TO 350 A.D.

IT was after the "Troubles" in the middle of the second century that a period of relative prosperity started for the native population of the north. The Brigantes had now a thriving tribal capital at Aldborough where the luxuries of Roman bath houses with tiles and decorated floors and with heating systems, and even shops and a games stadium, could be enjoyed. Romanised farmsteads were scattered over most of the best arable land of the county and trading posts and civilian towns with traders and craftsmen grew up outside the walls of the larger forts such as Ilkley and reached a very high development around York.

Even on the hill country of the Pennines smaller articles of Roman manufacture and coins became more frequent on all sites and suggest that there was now a growing, though still slender, intercourse between the hill tribes and the Roman soldier-police of the forts.

This quiet period was, however, fated not to outlast the century without an interruption, following the now common pattern. Political events in 193 A.D. starting with the assassination of Commodus and followed by many wranglings among the army chiefs and governors, led up to a war on the Continent to help which Britain was drained of some of her garrison.

The defeat and death of Claudius Albinus, Governor of Britain in 197, was the signal for a revolt of the northern tribes who broke through the defences of the Hadrianic Wall and with some of the Brigantes, wasted much of the northern province. Forts like Ilkley and Elslack were attacked and seriously damaged along with many others.

Nearly ten years were spent in rebuilding and repairing the forts and towns which suffered in that outbreak, but by the end of the opening decade of the third century the re-building was complete and the north entered again on a period of peace and prosperity which lasted for nearly a century. Recruits to the Roman Army were now partly drawn from the local peasantry instead of being brought entirely from other countries, so that it was now much easier to establish better relations between the army and native population.

During the third century Roman habits and fashions dominated the life of the Vale of York, centring around and between the military fortress of York and the civilian city of Aldborough. Aldborough covered nearly sixty acres and was surrounded by a massive wall of sandstone, the foundations of which are still preserved in part and vary in thickness between eleven and sixteen feet.

The houses were of timber, built on stone foundations, and some of the rooms were floored with tessellated pavements, many of which can be seen today. The floor in such cases was generally made with concrete, carefully levelled with a kind of mortar, then decorated in most elaborate patterns made up of "tesserae" or small square blocks of different coloured materials, red, brown, white and occasionally green, often less than an inch in size, arranged in a mosaic. Some of the patterns were strictly geometric, but others depicted scenes from mythology or had other devices. In one of the villas which will be mentioned later, that of Harpham in the East Riding, one of the tessellated pavements, uncovered nearly fifty years ago, shows a fine example of the true labyrinth drawn out in tesserae. This is a very ancient (long pre-Roman) device, and many examples are known to come from Crete and other places. In the form in which we see it here, the labyrinth motif has been found at Caerleon in a Roman house, and at several Roman sites on the Continent.

Many floors were heated by a hypocaust, a low basement of close-set pillars supporting the floor, between which pillars, hot air, and no doubt a lot of smoke and fume, circulated from a furnace. In some cases, like the villa near Middleham in Wensleydale, the remains of a hypocaust is the most certain evidence of the existence of a Roman house.

Within the town of Aldborough there were several public buildings and temples, and just outside the gates was a stadium for games and probably for athletic competitions. The population was mainly made up of Romanised Brigantes who had accepted Roman customs and rule, and there were probably some retired legionaries and some smaller officials also.

A much smaller civil settlement grew up around Brough on Humber, where the population was drawn largely from the parisii of East Yorkshire, but this town never attained the high degree of wealth and luxury that is to be deduced in Aldborough.

York was now one of the principal cities of the Province of Britain, but its military life was less rigid and formal than it had been, and many of the garrison and officers had homes within the fort in which they housed their families, while some others lived outside the fort in the civil settlements that were growing up in the area now known as Clifton, or across the river alongside the Tadcaster road.

This gave York a strong civilian flavour which was encouraged by the rapid growth of this civilian settlement across the river. After twenty years of service many of the legionaries took advantage of Roman custom and retired, and some were granted plots of land outside the fortress. These with traders and craftsmen, families and camp-followers, formed the nucleus of a civilian town centred round what is now Micklegate Bar and the Mount, and spreading out along the Tadcaster road as well. In the early part of the third century York became one of the four "Coloniae" in Britain, a community of ex-soldiers granted the privileges of Roman citizenship which they held by charter.

The importance of York is shown by the frequent visits paid to it by Emperors of Rome and the choice of York as the residence of some of the Governors of Roman Britain. Septimus Severus came to York after his campaign in Scotand and died there in 211 A.D.   Nearly a century later Constantine the Great was proclaimed at York as ruler of the western provinces of the Roman empire.   The city must thus have had a great dignity and importance in the eyes of the Romans, and this would be reflected in the importance, wealth and standard of living in the civil settlements around it.

The area of the fortress was a rectangle with its walls lying north-east to south-west and north-west to south-east. The western wall ran through the present Bootham Bar, which is on the site of the north gateway of the Roman fortress.   The Via Principalis, the main street of the Fort, was on the line of Petergate, though in the many subsequent rebuildings this street has diverged a little from the straight-ruled line of the Roman Street, and the east gate to which it ran, was in what is now Kings Square.

Stonegate is on the line of the cross street, Via Praetoria, from the south gate, and where the two crossed, just south of the south porch of the Minster, was the centre of the fortress. The commandant's house and other official buildings would flank the headquarters building and the legionary chapel or temple.   These were probably on the site now covered by the Minster, so that the Minster was probably founded in the seventh century on what had formerly been the pagan religious centre of Roman York.

The north-east wall of the fortress ran through Monk Bar and the south-west wall stretched parallel to the river, from the Multangular Tower (still standing), just north of Coney Street, to the south-east tower south of St. Sampsons Square.   Besides the usual military buildings the town included temples, shops, and some civilian houses.

One of the temples was dedicated to the god Serapis by Claudius Hieronymianus, legate of the sixth Legion, the Victorious. The dedication stone of this temple is illustrated and the inscription tells us that Hieronymianus built the temple from the ground up.   A wonderful collection of inscriptions, fragments of buildings, pottery and objects of all kinds is brought together in the Museum in the grounds of St. Mary's Abbey, in Lendal, York, and this ought to be seen and studied by everyone who takes interest in the past life of Yorkshire.

The worship of Serapis was only one of the many religions and cults that flourished in York, and among them Christianity had found a place by the fourth century, as the Council of Arles in 314 A.D. was attended by three bishops from Britain, one of whom was Eborius of York.

21

During the same period, the fort at Malton was experiencing less rigid military discipline and the excavations, few as they are, serve to indicate some infiltration of civilians into the life of the fort. In East Yorkshire there was a spread of civilian settlement over much new ground, and a type of settlement was founded which became the dominant feature of the next century, that of the villa.

The Roman word "villa" is used in this context to indicate a large farm which generally included a principal house, farm buildings, workshops and accommodation for a large number of servants and slaves or serfs. The farms were worked on a large scale and sent corn to the markets of such towns as York and Malton or to the Roman forts.

A very typical villa was settled near Rudston on a site which had been occupied in the first and second centuries by the Iron Age Parisii, probably as a small farm or homestead. In the third century the ditches of this earlier site were filled in and levelled off by means of a thick layer of gravel. The villa had several rooms in the main house, of which at least three had tessellated floors decorated in very intricate patterns. Beneath the footings of some of the walls, infants had been buried and these may represent some dedication ceremony or belief, but it would not be wise to jump to too easy a conclusion about this. Among the outside buildings were workshops and there was a large room which had contained several ovens for drying corn. The villa had been altered, extended and partly reconstructed at more than one date, but had evidently been the centre for a long time of intensive farming.

Most of the villas had a series of rooms arranged to open off a single corridor, or else they were set around the three sides of a courtyard. Several of the rooms and the corridor were floored with tiles or with tesserae, while some were heated by a hypocaust. In many of the villas which have been excavated the rubbish in the rooms includes coloured and patterned plaster from the walls as well as other evidence that the main house was built, decorated and furnished in very good style and was by no means a simple farm house. The outbuildings of a villa may often include a bath house which, like those of the forts, often has three baths, cold, warm and hot, and other small rooms as well. Workshops are generally present — corn drying kilns, barns and store-houses — and other typical farm structures. Many villa sites have first been discovered when in ploughing or by some other accident, part of a tessellated pavement has been revealed.

Villas were built in the rich alluvial ground of the River Aire at Kirk Sink, Gargrave; in Wensleydale near Middleham; and at Well and at North Stainey, on the west of the Vale of York. These were all occupied in the third century but were burned down at the opening of the fourth century between 300 and 304 A.D.  22

This destruction followed on the troubles of 290 A.D. when the forts at Ilkley and Bainbridge had been damaged and partly burned. This same trouble in an early stage is probably indicated at Malton where, soon after 280 A.D., the garrison collected together the stores of corn from their granaries, piled it against the rampart on the north-east side of the fort, just north of the gate and burned it. The evidence of this is seen in the layer of carbonised grain, often a foot thick, which was found in the recent excavations. The destruction of the stores preceded an evacuation of the fort for a time.

This disturbed period at the end of the third century was due in the first place to a new enemy. The tribes to the north of the Roman Wall were quiet, but in 287 A.D. the first pirates from across the North Sea harried the British coasts, and political unrest in the country increased this threat to peace. The title of Emperor in Britain was claimed by two usurpers, Allectus and Carausius, causing confusion during which some of the Roman garrison were withdrawn from the Wall, thus encouraging the northern tribes to make a southern sortie. York was threatened and in 296 A.D. the Emperor Constantius Chlorus came over to Britain to manage the situation.

Among his various measures was the repair and extensive reconstruction of the fortress at York, to which reconstruction the Multangular Tower belongs. The walls of the fortress facing the river were redesigned and largely rebuilt. Constantius Chlorus died at York in 306 A.D. after the completion of the reconstruction.

After this intrusion of trouble, the comparatively peaceful times returned and during the first half of the fourth century villas flourished over most of the lowland area of Yorkshire. On the Pennines many of the "Camps" — the Romano-British sites of the Iron Age fields and hutments — had their great expansion and in many of them, such as Grassington, and some of those near Settle, the fourth century pottery fragments are the most abundant remains.

Evidently life was a little easier and it seems possible that there was some trade between the hill tribes and the people of the plains, forts and villas; wool, skins or animals and occasional animals for food were exchanged for pots and small objects of various types.

It is in the early part of this fourth century that the contact between Romans and natives seems to have been at its greatest and friendliest stage. Once again however, there was unrest and trouble, and the later part of the century is concerned largely with the defence of the coast against the new raiders, the Saxon pirates and invaders from the Continent.

# 4. The Romans Leave Yorkshire

DURING the three centuries of Roman occupation already outlined, the centres of interest have swung off the Pennines into the Vale of York, from the military roads and forts of the highland zone to the farm lands and the civilian towns of the lowlands. In the last phase of the Roman story the interest moves to east Yorkshire and the coast, with the fort and town of Malton claiming the centre of the scene.

The earliest plans of the Romans in the North were dominated by the necessity to enclose and neutralise the resentful Brigantes and to maintain a barrier from which, as a base, the Picts to the north of the Wall could be pacified and controlled. Always the turbulent elements of the native population lay to the west and the north and time after time trouble descended on the country from those parts.

We have mentioned, however, that in the late third century trouble threatened from a new direction when in 287 A.D. the first Saxon pirates reached the east coast, although as yet their raids were litle more than tentative explorations. In 293 A.D. a military commander had been stationed at York under the title of Dux Britanniarum, charged with the duty of protecting the northern frontier. During the fourth century the pressure of the Teutonic invaders became serious, particularly on the south and east coasts and to meet it another new command was created with the title of Count of the Saxon Shore, and its holder was the organiser of coast defences and commander of the large forts which were now built to cope with the Saxon menace along the coast between the Wash and Beachy Head.

These measures were successful for a time but in 367 A.D. there was a simultaneous attack by Saxons on the coasts and Picts from north of the Wall, which was only defeated at the expense of heavy loss and destruction. Theodosius was put in charge of the restoration of the damage and much of the work done under his direction can be recognised and is noted by inscriptions at many places in the North; Ilkley and Malton were partly restored by him but much of the work was very shoddy stuff.

This Theodosian plan included the erection of Malton to a new importance, as the centre from which to control and direct a scheme of coast protection. Along the Yorkshire coast from the Tees estuary to Filey, and most probably further south to Lincolnshire and the Wash and north to the Tyne, a chain of signal towers was built, from which a watch could be kept against attack from the sea. From Flamborough Head as far south as the Wash, coast erosion has removed a strip of land estimated to reach a maximum of three miles wide in Holderness. This probably accounts for the lack of any traces on the present coast. These signal stations were linked with Malton and York and the main garrisons were so placed as to be able to pass visible signals from one to the other right along the line of the coast and also to the inland forts.

Part of the Roman fleet was stationed on the Humber so that in the event of an attack, the fleet could be called out and directed and troops could be summoned and moved from York and Malton to any part of the coast. This idea of signal stations was no new one, as Dr. Richmond has recently brought forward evidence that the small Roman sites which stand close to the road across Stainmoor are part of such a line of signal stations from York to the western end of the Roman Wall.

One of these sites is only about twenty yards north of the present road at 250 yards east of Bowes Moor Hotel (New Spital). It is a rectangular earth rampart, sixty feet by forty-seven overall, with the rampart ten feet wide having a narrow entrance in the south side. Outside the rampart there is a V-shaped ditch also ten feet wide, with the earth thrown up as an outer bank. An almost exactly similar earthwork is seen at Roper Castle on Stainmoor south of Rey Cross, and at the western tip of Stainmoor the small fort of Maiden Castle carries the line forward to the Roman Station of Veterae at Brough.

Three other sites in this line have been identified in the Vale of Eden, while on the east the line would be carried by Bowes, Greta Bridge, Catterick and other stations, to York. Each site is in clear view of its two neighbours and Richmond suggests that a tall semaphore tower or mast on each was used pretty much as a field telephone would be used today, for urgent and immediate instructions.

The date of these Stainmoor signal stations is suggested as second century, following the rebellion of 155-158 A.D., but pottery and coins at Maiden Castle continue the date into the last quarter of the fourth century and it is likely that this line was again used in the same time as the line along the coast, and may in fact have been the model for the construction of the signal stations.

The system of signal stations along the coast has left prominent remains easily visited, at Huntcliff, Goldsborough, Peak, Scarborough and Filey. The best displayed of these is the signal station at Scarborough within the grounds of the Castle. This was excavated in 1922-24 and was left fully exposed. The building is 150 feet square with a stone wall of which the corners are rounded, each corner having an external D-shaped hollow bastion on which a catapult was probably placed.

The excavators judged from the structure and the amount of material that the wall had been about twenty feet high. Outside the wall there is a level strip or berm, thirty feet wide, then a V-shaped ditch. In the centre of the building there are the foundations of a tower on top of which would be the semaphore. The tower foundations were fifty feet square and four courses of masonry are still in position.

The tower was of many storeys and the first floor beams were supported by wooden posts, the bases of which were revealed by the excavation. It is suggested from the strength of the foundations that this tower could have been seventy or eighty feet high. The garrison of forty local militia men lived in the tower as there are no other buildings around it. At Filey the signal station is on the headland, Carr Naze, just at the narrowest point so that two of the walls have been lost by the cliff erosion, but the other two remain. Excavators have discovered the socket stones into which the pillars supporting the first floor were fitted, and also some pottery and coins, which help in the dating. In the last excavation of 1921 two hoards of coins were found which are dated about 395 A.D.

The next signal station north of Scarborough is at the Peak, Ravenscar, but very little is known of the details of this as its site is covered by the Raven Hall Hotel. When the foundations for this building were dug in 1774 an inscribed stone was found (now in Whitby Museum) which can be translated "Justinianus the Commander Vindicianus — the prefect of Soldiers built this fort."

Goldsborough, still further north, stands back a quarter of a mile from the coast, on a low hill just near Kettleness station, and overlooking Runswick Bay. This is in strong contrast with the next station at Huntcliff, a mile to the east of Saltburn, which is perched on the very edge of a high sea cliff.

The two stations are identical in size and plan — a five feet thick sandstone wall encloses a square of 105 feet side, with a bastion at each corner. The ditch is thirty feet wide and five feet deep, with a wide berm between it and the wall. The central tower was forty-five feet square and within it were the bases of the first floor supporting pillars.

The finds from Huntcliff include a number of coins which date the occupation to the short period about 370-395 A.D Many personal ornaments were found incuding two bronze brooches and a jet ring. The pottery was of a late fourth century type to which the site has given its name, so that similar pottery from many parts of the North and from the Roman Wall, is referred to as Huntcliff ware. In the well, just inside the court, there were many bones, mainly of women and children, and also a piece of brown cloth.

There is plenty of evidence here as at other stations, of the violence and cruelty of the piratical raids which closed the fourth century and eventually overthrew the signal stations.

These signal stations were part of an interlinked system which depended upon Malton and eventually on York for the forces which could counter an invasion, and Malton, during the last quarter of the fourth century was indeed the nerve centre and hub of the military life of east and north Yorkshire. At the same time, under the protection of this system there was a prosperous and very widespread civilian life with a great expansion in the number of wealthy villas and farms, and a thriving civilian town just outside the fort of Malton.

The roads necessary for the speedy movement of troops to any threatened part of the coast, opened up the whole country to easy movement and the large garrisons of soldiers and the thriving towns created markets to which goods and food were carried from all directions. Many of the villas were rebuilt on more lavish lines or extended, and new ones were occupied, such as the large corridor house at Langton, the extended house at Rudston, the villa at Brantingham and others.

The civilian town at Malton lay on the south bank of the Derwent, under the area now covered by the suburb of Norton, and was connected with the fort by an important ford by which several roads approached the south east gate. Finds of pottery, coins, personal ornaments and many burials are evidence of the size of this settlement. An inscription found early in the nineteenth century can be translated "Greeting to the Spirit of this place. My servant, good luck to your goldsmith's shop" and this suggests that some degree of luxury and wealth existed to support this and other craftsmen.

Besides the goldsmith and other trades, this suburb of Malton was the centre of the pottery industry, as well as glass making, and during the late fourth century Malton was in fact a centre around which several potteries flourished and from which pots were sent to most of the Roman stations in the North. One of the potteries was discovered in 1923 by a boy from Bootham School, and was excavated during the following years. This was a site on the Cram Beck at its junction with the Derwent, near Castle Howard station.

There is a good seam of suitable clay and on a site well above the beck four kilns were found. These consist of a keyhole-shaped structure, a circular stoke hole at one end feeds a flue leading from it through a furnace or kiln trench, covered by perforated clay slabs.

Another group of kilns was found in the East Riding at Throlam near Home-on-Spalding Moor, and these followed a similar plan. The pottery produced was a hard material, black or bluish-grey, generally well burnished, and occasionally showing signs that some of it may have been painted. Bowls and dishes were produced in large numbers along with jars of many sizes.

The heaviest ware was the mortarium, or mortar in which food was crushed and when we remember that pulse and ground-up corn were the principal foods of the Romans we can understand the frequency with which portions of mortaria are found in nearly all excavations. As the pottery is found both on military sites and in villas and other civilian settlements, even in some of the hill villages around Settle and Grassington, it is certain that the pottery was carried to the civilian markets as well as being supplied to the forts.

In the Vale of York and the eastern hills the native population was steadily becoming more Romanised and as more native militia were recruited to replace Roman soldiers the clear separation of Roman and Briton became much less obvious and a population more truly Romano-British developed.

This country was, however, more than ever dependent upon Roman organisation for its protection from the invaders from east and north, and as the Roman garrisons were reduced at the beginning of the fifth century, the Romano-British population was left in a sad predicament.

Again we have to look at the Continent for the conditions which weakened the Roman rule and which encouraged the "barbarian" invasions of the west. The abandonment of Hadrian's Wall in 383 A.D. had not any immediate serious consequences for the North, but five years later there was another period of plotting and unrest on the Continent. Maximus was defeated and in 395 A.D. Theodosius left his eleven-year-old son, Honorius, as ruler of the western empire, with his general Stilicho as Regent, while he went to deal with the troubles in Rome. Raids by Picts, Scots and Saxons naturally followed but were defeated in 400 A.D.

Trouble on the Continent increased and Stilicho took more troops from Britain, seriously reducing all its defences. The old story of intrigues and jealousies among the rival factions for the Governorship was repeated throughout the next ten years, during which time in 406 A.D. the Goths moved south across the Rhine and in 410 A.D. sacked the city of Rome. There were still a few Roman troops in Britain but they had no commander and were powerless against the northern invaders.